Pivot

Pivot

Quiana Malone

Edited by Michael Goldsmith

SISTER & SAMPSON
PUBLISHING

2019

First Printing: 2019

ISBN 978-1-7323699-3-1

Library of Congress Control Number: 2019902980

Sister & Sampson Publishing, LLC
Jacksonville, FL 32236
www.sisterandsampsonpublishing.com

Ordering Information:

Special discounts are available on quantity purchases by corporations, associations, educators, and others. For details, contact the publisher at the above listed address.

U.S. trade bookstores and wholesalers:

Please contact Sister & Sampson Publishing

Email sisterandsampsonpublishing@gmail.com

Dedication

To my son Nick.

All your dreams are possible. Live your dreams!

Contents

Acknowledgements

Writing a book is NOT as easy as one would think; however, it is gratifying. The process to get the content together presented challenges as well. The person I'm most appreciative of is my son, Nicholas Parker, Jr., for being my inspiration and my motivation for everything!

I want to thank Devin D. Coleman, for the push to do things the right way and not just settling for mediocre or good enough concerning this project. The pushback wasn't meant to be difficult, but I had to accept that sometimes a challenge is strictly for enhancement – enhancement means turning something good into something great!

I also thank Miranda Thomas, Danielle Lewis, and Audriana Malone for being my sounding boards and friends I needed to make it through this journey. What's understood doesn't need to be explained when it comes to you three.

Preface

piv·ot /def/

The central point, pin, or shaft on which a mechanism turns or oscillates.

That's what you could call my life and all the obstacles that it took for me to get to the place of a Pivot. What do you call the girl who was born to be great but the only success she found solace in was messing up? Being a teenage mother, in and out of incarceration, and just making all the wrong decisions.

Pivot tells a story about a young lady who accepted everything that wasn't meant for her until she decided that she was going to go after everything that was! *Pivot* is a funny, direct, and graphic story of how you can be whatever you want to be, even after you have been what everyone considered you to be for so long.

This book takes you on her journey, starting from the day she was released from a horrendous yet humbling prison sentence to the place where she decided she was built – and ready – for change. As you turn each page, understand that who she was then, and all the things she has gone through, has been the very thing that makes her the woman she is now!

Chapter 1

January 14, 2010. As I was lying on the top bunk in my dorm, all I could hear was "PACK IT UP!"

Those are the golden words that every inmate would love to hear, but for me, I was in disbelief, absolute shock. I wasn't looking to leave this place until April. I walked up to the guard at the gate, and before I could say anything, she said, "You want to stay or are you going to get your stuff to get out of here?" Asking no questions, I turned around to empty my locker clean, got all my books and essential letters off the table, and proceeded to the door. Everybody was congratulating me and telling me to never return. I didn't belong in there, and I was the one they were looking forward to hearing from the most when they got out. For as long as I've been interacting with people, I have always been told, "You are the one we depend on." But I NEVER believed it!

Walking to the releasing hold, I heard one of the guards say, "Girl, you are lucky." I stopped and pivoted, asking "Why?" at the same time.

"These people like you in here" was the reply. "They went back to look and see how long you had left and found out that you were sentenced before the new 85% guidelines took effect. So Classification made adjustments to your release date to effect the 65% that you were sentenced under."

I thought to myself, "Thank God I got myself together when I did." When I first arrived and was assigned the job detail, I hated it and refused to do the work, which resulted in my first DR. Unbeknownst to me it, was never filed – just used as a tactic to scare me. To this day, I wonder why Ms. Brown never submitted it. I guess she saw something in me, too, and held out hope that I would become something better one day.

Ms. Brown and I knew each other from the street. We didn't have a good taste for one another. I knew her lifestyle, and she knew mine, it was mutual respect: I wouldn't tell your secrets, and you wouldn't tell my business. In the beginning, we didn't see eye to eye. I think it was because neither of us knew if the other would have that mutual respect, but after a few weeks had passed and nothing came from either side, the pact was set. She ended up being a pretty good ally. She would let me go in last if I was on my menstruation. She acted as if she needed me to stay after and help her out so that I wouldn't have to drop and squat in front of over fifty other women that had to take a shower and get to the chow hall before 4 pm when dinner was served. I didn't necessarily get to shower by myself, and I still had to squat and cough, but it wasn't in front of as many people. I was in good with the guards, so they would let me and my blood be handled with a little bit more privacy. Imagine having to stand in line with a whole bunch of other women, removing every stitch of clothing you have, squatting and coughing to make sure that you are not bringing any contraband in the facility. Nasty, right?

As I continued to walk to the release center, all I could think about was how I was going to get home – nobody knew I was out. For the life of me, I could only think of two people to call, neither being family. I was able to use the phone, so I called the one person I couldn't wait to connect with on the outside – well, one of the people I was ready to see – and that was my homegirl, T. She had gotten out a few weeks before me and we just knew it would be months before we laid eyes on each other again. Before I could say anything, she was screaming, "They let you out!" I was like, "Whoa, whoa, how do you know?" Someone else we knew had come home early as well, so when she heard my voice and not the operator, she knew I was out. "I'm coming to get you. I'll be there in an hour."

Now, it usually took an hour and a half, but I knew she was coming on two wheels...

Chapter 2

In the car, all I did was look at the trees. It took a moment to register that I was finally free again. As I heard that gate creak closed behind me, some type of fear began to set in: where would I go? I had no money, no job, no car, and basically no one who cared. The ones who I thought would and could have my back were barely making it themselves.

I heard T talking to me and it snapped me back into reality. She was like, "You don't hear me!" Honestly, I didn't. I was too busy worrying about what would happen next. "Where we headed after I take you to get something to wear?"

Something to wear! I forgot that I had on two-year-old clothes and that I was two times smaller than I was when I last had these clothes on. Damn, that was something else to think about: where were all my things I left behind? I knew they were packed away somewhere, but where? And were they still in good condition? I always, ALWAYS liked nice things, and even though I hadn't home for a while and should really be grateful for whatever I had at that point, I still had a reputation to uphold. I wasn't about to go anywhere looking any kind of way.

We were about to hit the avenues when I heard T say, "No, no, no…we need to go over here off Lem Turner. What's over there? O naw we can't go yet. You don't want him to see you like that. You need to clean up first. Besides, nobody even knows you are home."

"I dooooooon't care, take me to Lem Turner so I can see my baby."

"You know what, you right. You talk about that man from sunup to sundown. What was I thinking?"

"Baby, I don't know what you were thinking, but I what I do know is we need to get there."

As I approached the driveway, the tears just started rolling.

"You crying already? You haven't even gotten to the door yet."

"I know it, man, but do you know how long it's been? He probably don't even remember me."

"Girl, you tripping. How can he not remember you? Man, get out and go in there and see that man and stop all that crying, acting worse than him."

We both laughed as I got out the car and walked inside. The lady at the front desk acted as if she saw a ghost. Then she reached up, smiled at me, ran from around the desk, and gave me a hug.

She took me directly to where she knew I wanted to go. As I walked into the quiet room, I heard the ladies all whispering and telling Nick to get up. As he got up, he looked around and then spotted me. We locked eyes with each other, but he didn't move. In my mind, I'm like, "I knew he wouldn't remember me." Before the thought in my mind could be complete, he ran over to me.

"Mommy, Mommy!"

My whole soul broke. I was so happy to see that boy. Oh my god, I was so glad to see him. We hugged for what felt like twenty minutes, but in reality was only two. He latched onto me and just began to talk, talk, talk. I swear, that was the highlight of my whole day. The release was great, but seeing my baby meant so much more.

Chapter 3

My incarceration took a toll on my whole family. I have a sister who was about fourteen or fifteen years old at the time, I can't really remember. Next to my son, she was my everything. Leaving her to have to fend pretty much for herself was very hard. When I arrived at my grandfather's house where she was staying, along with my son and my mother, she wasn't there. She was in high school, so she would be home soon.

Now, T was ready to go to the mall, but I was ready to go and see my people. "Hey T, just drop me off here and I'll get up with you later. I'm going to spend time with my son." The mall and anything it had could wait until later. No doubt I was going to get dead fresh before I saw some people, but at that time, Nick and Audri were all I really was interested in seeing.

"I'll call you when I'm on the way back to pick you up."

"All right, let me give you the house number." (I remembered it – how can anybody forget that number? It had been the same for forty years.) Walking up to the door, I heard my granddaddy on the phone telling somebody he hears someone outside and to hold on so he can get up to see. When he walked to the door and saw me, the first thing he said was, "You didn't break out of there, did you? Do I need to hide you?" He always had jokes.

I told him that I was released early. Being a very religious man, he swore on how GOOD God was, and I agreed. I guess he forgot he was on the phone or didn't care, because he didn't go back to that phone call for a while.

That was the beginning that I didn't know would turn my whole life around…

Chapter 4

Coming home this time was different. I think it was because it was after such a long time. I had been incarcerated on many occasions before, but not for this amount of time. Learning so much while I was locked up – much of what I had already known but getting more in-depth and actually having proof to back it up – brought me home with a different agenda than before. I came home feeling like I had something to prove. In every other situation before, I just did a day, a week, or a month or two, and I was back out to the same old thing – just finding what I thought were better ways of not getting caught. This time I vowed to be done, and I almost was…until I encountered what I'll call my first "frenemy".

I met her while I was locked up. Honestly, I was glad to share some of my time with a familiar face. She was a friend of the family, which kind of meant she was family to me, too. When we first saw each other, it was all love. We were both happy to have family in the pen. We were even lucky enough to be on the same work assignment and be in the same dorm. How ironic – I was thanking God every day, feeling like He had looked out for me. That was my first lesson that the Devil was just as capable as God, but I wasn't listening. It looked like God to me…how else could that happen, right?

We spent lots and lots of time together. She had been in for months before me, so she knew the ropes and was teaching me – I mean, incarceration was incarceration, but this was far better than the county prison to me. We began to do everything together. I was her shoulder, and she was mine. It was almost as if we were best friends. Everybody knew we rolled together, and if it didn't require two, then you definitely couldn't do anything with one. We kept everything new: every experience we had or created started from us, just as it wasn't one created by a mutual party, but one we created. That was until the day she said, "They was lying about all the things they said about you."

Now, today I know when I hear those words to haul ass, because there is definitely some bull crap and DRAMA to follow. Anybody who can tell what was told to them in privacy just to make conversation or gain a friend is not one to be trusted. Of course, I learned the hard way, but at any rate, the words were said and my interest was piqued. It was the first seed that was planted and I was ready to water it, so of course I asked what was said and who said it. That was her gateway to run her mouth like a faucet. And that she did! It was so much that almost everything she said was true, except the things said about my son.

When it came to my son, it seemed like everybody had an opinion. I was young and my son's father was much older. Of course, you couldn't tell me anything – I was in what I thought was love. There was always some controversy regarding the two of us. Mostly, I knew this to be true but refused to see, and some was just speculation. And you know, when YOUR home isn't right, it would only be right that MINE wasn't either. Another lesson: watch who brought you the bone, especially if they have no bones of their own. But I digress.

The things she told me hurt me to the core – like, really? Family talked about you like this when they weren't around you? Really? The fact that everything was true was even more devastating. I mean, it was no military secret that my mom had once been a victim of cocaine. (My girl has been clean for years now – isn't God good?) But to tell the stories that I had forced myself to forget – the same stories that you had to live yourself – were just despicable. Who would do that, just to have conversation? The family she spoke of were some of those I hold nearest and dearest to my heart. I looked up to them and I was always trying to find a way to fit in – mistake number one. I just couldn't understand it. Taking a bite out of reality isn't always easy, but such is life, right?

That wasn't the only information that was given, but it was enough. It was the first incident that made me start thinking and handling things differently. I was always the one to hold everything then blow up at the wrong time, and yea my blowups are huge. I obtained the name Hellraiser from it…funny, huh? Not I hated to be that way or that person, but I was still doing it. The same people who talked about me were the only ones to make consistent visits. I always wanted to deny them, but hell, it's always good to see somebody sitting at that table across from you. I always wanted to say something, but I just couldn't. I always wanted to hear the latest tea once every two weeks. I was always fortunate to have a visit every week (my best friends would alternate every week coming to see me). I never wanted my son to come. I couldn't take that.

I had made up my mind that I wasn't even going to say anything, but I would just know how to handle them accordingly. What was funny to me was, after every visit, my homie wanted to know what was said. When I was going to say something, that was red flag number two, but I just didn't see it. Or maybe it was that I didn't want to. It was as if she was looking to break a bond that was so tightly wound. I found out that was she was very possessive and territorial, and I was becoming a part of her territory. That sounds crazy, but hey, it does happen.

Chapter 5

Finally being free after being left behind for three months after my homegirl left was tough, but doable. I had, and then lost, the one person I was supposed to be able to lean on but I did do it – I made it out the gate. Coming home was one of the happiest days of my life, but it turned out to be one of the most trying times. It was trying because I had nothing. I mean, absolutely nothing. During my incarceration, I had lost everything.

I still feel guilty to this day for the way things went down when I left: leaving my sister behind to have to fend for herself and pick up unnecessary habits needed to survive just didn't sit well with me. It was my responsibility to make sure that she was okay. How could I leave her out here to fend for herself when I knew what she was left with and the condition she was left in? I now realize I dealt with a lot of selfishness, as we all do, even though it doesn't look like it at the time. We call it doing what we have to do, but for who? You never think about all the people it will affect. It's just what I needed at that moment to make me feel the way I needed to feel. I always used to say that I would "get me, me" by any means necessary, and most times that's what I did, no matter the cost.

Having no place to live was a huge deal for me. I always, ALWAYS had my own and took care of me and mine – there it is again: I always got me, me! I remember having a conversation with my grandfather, where he told me to stay at his house as long as I needed to, but to promise him I would get a job, save my money, and make sure to never go back to jail again. He didn't want anything from me, but honestly, for me to leave his house the right way – that whole conversation went in one ear and out of the other.

You see, we didn't have the best relationship. He always left me and my sis out as kids. He claimed that we were too privileged. He said that my mom did too much for us and that we were spoiled, so what he did for the rest of his grands he didn't do for us. How messed up is it to go to his house on Christmas and everybody getting savings bonds and jewelry boxes, and the nigga got me some pencils? Yea, I remember, and it stuck with me for a long time. So I would always be respectful – he was my senior, but attached I was NOT. He was who he was. His name was Granddaddy, so that's what I called him. I took everything coming from him with a grain of salt.

It's funny, though – when we finally talked about it twenty years later, what he told me made sense a lot of sense, but as a kid I wasn't feeling it. I came to find out he loved the way I did whatever I had to do, and that I never used him as a scapegoat. He said he always knew I would be the person I am today, and to ensure that I did, he used tough love. It amazes me how everybody saw me as being so damn tough, but to me I was dying inside, reaching and acting out, looking for somebody, anybody to care.

So no place, no clothes, NOTHING.

Chapter 6

After my release, of course, me and my homie were still down. She waited on me and had a whole setup for me when I came home. Now that was love there, right? There was a three-month gap between our releases, so she had a chance to get out and make a couple of moves before I touched down. I didn't see her struggle – all I saw was the aftermath, not even knowing I was her motivation. I looked at and paid more attention to what I saw. I don't think I ever stopped to think and assess, I just saw. Pride was a major part of my demise, and coming out, there was no way in hell I was staying with my grandfather and my mom and my sister and my uncle and whoever else when they needed somewhere to stay. Besides, we lived in the hood, in less-than-favorable conditions, but we knew how to make it work. There were some cold-ass winters and some scorching-ass summers. I couldn't do another season like that.

On the streets again, I know I said I was going straight and narrow, but the people that needed me knew I needed them. They knew I had lost everything before I did, so when I touched down, they were looking for me, ready to get me right. And I was ready, praying the whole way. I made it to Miami and back in one day. I had things to do and an image to reset. I remember going to get my hair done and giving the girl my very last – I didn't have a dime left, but what I did have was my hair done.

To me, my son had been neglected because he didn't have the latest. I hated taking him to school and he wasn't caught up. "Give me a month, son," is what I remember telling him. To be honest, he didn't give a damn. He was just happy to have me home. I couldn't see that, though, All I saw was trend and status.

Running back and forth for a while started causing stress in all my relationships. I ended up bumping heads with my homie and our relationship became strained, but it was eventually going to happen, and I knew it. She was the "what I did for you" type, and I was the total opposite.

Now, I was a trip – I mean a whole vacation – but my heart has always been PURE, so anything I ever did was from the heart. On top of that, I was still a big giver and a sucker for happiness. I've taken the L many times just to keep peace, never realizing strength I possessed. I could take a lot of what others couldn't even take an ounce of. I always exuded the very thing I couldn't see – some people loved that about me, but most hated it and couldn't understand it.

My grandfather told me he knew what I was doing and that I couldn't do that from under his roof. Now, what I was trying to figure out was, how in the world did he know that I was back into the same old thing? I knew he kept his ear to the street, but dang, he could tell me what I was doing and who I was doing it with. I thought I was being more discreet and low-key, and I wasn't even staying at his house since stepping back out into the streets.

I had been staying with my homie. She had kids, but they loved me, and her guy had just caught some time, so it was like we needed each other. Most times I was gone, and as much as I was away from my son, you would think that I would be more grounded. But again, my thinking was fucked up. I thought that by grinding and making up for lost time through materialistic things, I was doing something. In reality, he was feeling worse than he did when I was in!

There was a conversation I had with my grandfather that I remember to this day. When he found out I was back into what I was before, he told me he couldn't be mad at me, but he was disappointed. He wasn't mad wholly, because I was much like him when he was younger. I was going to get it by any means necessary, and until I found my own reasoning, there would be none. Now, I heard him and took it for what it was worth, but at the same time I had been home for months by that point – and no one had offered me anything but some lame-ass advice that they couldn't take themselves. I listened, but I wouldn't apply it until way later.

Chapter 7

Moving out wasn't hard at all. I never really had anything there. We moved to an apartment on the north side, tucked off on Harts Road. It was decent – actually, it was more than I expected. I didn't have anything, but hell, I was out on my own. Slowly but surely, we fixed it up and turned it into a magazine spread. I like nice things – rather, it was what I was wearing or what I was living in. At that point I was utterly SOLO.

I rekindled a relationship with one of my best friends from high school. She was a friend – not a buddy, but a friend. You know, with a buddy, it's everyday – y'all hanging, you-don't-see-one-without-the-other type of deal. But a friend, it could be months or years but you're always able to pick right up where you left off with no discrepancies. I had her back and she had mine. That was my nigga right there. We started hanging real tight and she was at my house more than me. My little sister came to live with me and that was golden. I had missed being able to dictate what she did and where she went. It was all love, though. She had landed a job and was doing well for herself. I was super proud. I still felt super guilty about leaving her, so I always made sure she had the best of everything, and every chance I got, I spoiled the hell out of her. I think I've added a little to the stress her husband catches to this day. There were so many fun days as well as bad days in that apartment. If the walls could talk, they would have a story to tell from my secrets being exposed to me having to fight for my life.

There was this guy. We were only friends – I mean the best of friends – but one day something just happened. I ended up on my back with his head between my legs. Of course, it was on from then. It was like we couldn't get enough of each other. He would tell me about his now-wife and I would tell him about my now-ex. We were kind of forbidden to mess around, but it was a secret we kept for over a year. One thing about what's done in the dark: it ALWAYS comes to the light eventually. I had a cousin who came into town, and they were cool. We were at a party, and unbeknownst to him, he ratted us out. It made things hella awkward between some, but not us. I actually laughed, like, "Damn, I guess they know." I say some because he was hella handsome and I wasn't the only one that was trying to get that, but I was the successful one. Hell, it wasn't supposed to happen like that, but it did. I was always kind of secretive when it came to any endeavors or affairs. I'm actually still that way. Some call it sneaky…I say I'm keeping people out of my business.

I had to fight my way out of there a time or two. Also, I wasn't for any man putting his hand on me, and I let it be known straight up! I guess he felt like he was different, or I was the same. I had gotten in a relationship that, in the beginning, was really sweet, but then went crazy as hell. I kind of knew he was crazy when I started talking to him. but it was like I was chasing a thrill. He was a good dude, but he had a mean streak – it took me awhile to see it, but when I did, I did. There was one only one fight, and that was it. I'm not a fighter, but I definitely know how to do it, and he wasn't accustomed to women who fight back. It was as if he got off on beating the hell out of women. Nope, not for me, though – as soon as the first hit was thrown, it was on. What was funny was the fact that after the lick, was returned – he bowed up at me and said, "Oh, you want to fight back!" It was at that point that I knew this nigga was crazy as hell. After we damn near killed each other, I knew it was a wrap. This nigga had to GO!

Lesson learned: if the nigga shows you a sign of being crazy, then nine times out of ten, he is crazy, and you need to pass by his ass!

Chapter 8

I was soon working at the County Jail. One of the best jobs that I had ever had, if you ask me, I was what we call "now living my best life". I had all the power and they especially hated the ones that knew the real me and knew that I really had no business being there. One in particular was Officer Ramirez. He hated me and everything I stood for. He had great reason, too.

It's funny how things come back around full circle. A few years prior, Officer Ramirez was a corrections officer at the facility I was housed. He was one of the cocky dudes who though that because he looked halfway decent, he could get whatever he wanted from whom-ever he wanted…WRONG! We had quite a few run-ins. My mouth has always gotten me into trouble in one way or another. See, he liked to catch you by yourself and push up on you or come at you in a way to see if he could. We had our episode and I wasn't with it at all – first of all, I never had a thing for anything other than black men, and sec-ond, I was there to do my time and that was it. Anything I wanted I could buy, and I didn't need any bribe or extra credit to get it.

What he didn't know was the reason I rarely made small talk with too many people or them with me. He tried the friendly approach at first, and based on his response to mine, he didn't know that I wasn't really that either. Soon enough, he found out that I wasn't one to be joking or trying to make bribes with, and that left a bad taste in his mouth for me. Little did either of us know, we would see each other again.

"This is Officer Ramirez." I was introduced to him on my first day as being my go-to. The look on his face was priceless. I just simply smiled and extended my hand out to him. He reluctantly took it and followed suit. It wasn't until he caught me alone, which seemed to never happen – in the quad, all eyes were always everywhere un – until my schedule changed. I had to now be in from 2 AM until 12 PM each day. This was a gift and a curse.

"How in the hell did you get in here?"

"What do you mean?" I asked him. "I work here. You see me every day I don't understand what you are asking me." I had a way of being facetious. He hated it.

"Cut the shit, you know exactly what I'm talking about. Did they run a background check on you?"

Now it was my turn. "No, you cut the shit. You know damn well they did a background check on me, the same way they did one on you. All that matters is I'm here. You stay out of my way and I'll stay out of yours. I don't have an issue, as long as you keep that smartass mouth to yourself."

He couldn't stand the thought that I was now his equal and there wasn't a damn thing he could do about it. Honestly, I had no idea how I landed this gig. My stepmother, who was a C.O, told me to apply. I did, and I was hired. I didn't know what strings she pulled, neither did I care. I was there and that was that.

Having to be to work at 2 AM was good because I had most of my days and some of my nights to do what I needed to do. It was also hell, though, because I was a party animal. I went out almost every day of the week and lived for the weekend. I would leave the club and go straight to work. The thing was, I wasn't leaving the club in time to get to work – I was leaving after the time I was supposed to be there. It just wasn't right if I left the club before the two o'clock ride out. I just couldn't do it, so I didn't do it. Nobody ever said anything because I always had my work done and a few inmates I could depend on, I had it so sweet that even the corrections officer working the gate would already have gone down to the part and let the trustees in the basement for me. Everybody knew their respective job and place and they went there and did what they were supposed to do until I got there.

Just like anything else, all good things eventually come to an end. I wasn't not only disliked by Officer Ramirez, but the other workers as well, solely because I could get my guys to do what they couldn't get them to do. The reality was that I just treated them like they were somebody. Of course, I could understand them because I was just like them. It wasn't long before they set me up to get fired out of there. I was accused of letting one of the inmates use the phone. Now, even the inmate who they stated I had let in the quad denied it, but it was their word against mine. I didn't get let go but moved to another facility where I didn't want to be, so I quit.

Still, to this day, when I see Ramirez, he swears he didn't have anything to do with it, and that he believed me. The thing is, I didn't believe him, and he knew it. He also knew I didn't care. Countless times, I've had to tell him to save his apologies. Because I didn't need them.

Chapter 9

Leaving that job kind of left me back at square one, but not really. I could have easily found another one, but why? I knew what I could do to get some money and fast. At that time, I was running with the wrong company and got sucked into a lifestyle I'm not really proud of, but hey, at the time, it was what it was. I started scamming and kind of lost sight of everything that mattered and what made sense. Right and wrong had been long gone, and I was just living for me and my boy, and luckily, I never got caught. Before my senses came back, I always thought that scamming was just bottom-of-the-barrel, like it wasn't a real hustle. I wasn't necessarily hurting anybody but myself because I was using my own info. It was just the way I was switching it up and using it. I started selling weed, but that was like pennies to me, so that didn't last long, either. Getting another job seemed like the only reasonable thing to do, so that's what I did. I worked for a while, but I didn't like the job and walked right off it with no explanation. I dared anyone to ask me where I was going.

A couple of months went by with me just doing me and making it how I made it. I had started hanging out with my homegirl again, and I guess you know I was back in knee-deep again this time. I was calling the shots. I had finessed so many people previously, and they loved my prices and the way I moved. I had begun to buy my own, break it down, and just get off of it like I wanted, cutting out the mid-dle- and front-men. I was the whole deal.

Now, I had been dibbling and dabbling the whole time. I was working, but I was moving for someone else – basically just paying attention and learning what I needed to know. Some people got a kick out of the fact that I was a female who knew how to move just as smooth as a nigga, so they messed with me heavy. They didn't want to mess with anybody but me. There were some who were mostly intimidated by females, but there were also some dudes who wanted me way out the way.

I started learning how to make my own way from an old head who respected me. We would sit up all night talking about money and listening to music. That man loved Prince. It was weird trapping all night, listening to Prince, getting the game, and making money. He was family, so it was nothing but love. Some nights, it was just me coming up off what I had but really watching the way the other niggas moved in his absence. He Trusted nobody, and after a while, life would prove why he didn't, and I didn't either.

One night in that spot changed my life forever – I mean, I was grown, so I knew what it was, but to actually come face-to-face with the very thing I prayed so hard against was hard as hell. I heard a familiar voice walking up to the door. There was no light, but I always sat in a spot where I could see and not be seen. My homie had already peeped game and tried to intercept, but it was too late. I had already seen her, and she had seen me. The messed-up part was that she didn't even turn to walk away. She came to get what she came for and she didn't give a damn who she saw. My people were with her and he turned away, but hell, for what? If he didn't care, why should you?

But he did. I didn't know whether to cry or curse. I chose to curse, unphased and really falling on deaf ears. That night messed my whole world up. I was pissed, not only at her, but at everybody I was looking at. Everybody that was there on a regular basis. "This been going on and y'all didn't tell me. Why were y'all were even serving her?" That was the million-dollar question. Nobody could give me answers. All I saw was low-hung heads and muted mouths. I was madder at my family, though. Nigga, how could you?

I stopped showing up and stopped answering his phone calls for about a week. He caught up with me, though: "What's up, cuz?" I kept going. I didn't have anything to say, so he said it all. His reasoning was the addiction – the addiction, no matter who fed it. It was either him or the nigga next door. It made sense and was very true, but my reasoning was, "out of sight, out of mind". I knew what was happening, but I didn't care to see it. Hell, his people were the same, but on a different side of town, so it was easier for him than it was for me. We ran in the same circles and on the same grounds. I didn't give a damn how he put it. I wasn't with it, and no matter how true it was, it wasn't making sense to me.

Until one night. Everything had blown over and I was back in the spot again. And I'll be damned, here they came again, brother and sister looking for what they were looking for.

Something in me changed. It's as if a replay of my life for the last seven years just played right before me: "I see you get up to go to work every day just to do this – I mean you had a house and a car.

You kept nice things, but for some reason, you couldn't shake this shit and didn't seem to want to."

There I was, putting every ounce of freedom I had into a jeopardizing position to take care of my responsibility and yours, while helping the dope man get rich. Nope, wasn't going to happen. If anybody was going to come up, it was going to be me, so I did what would haunt me for the rest of my life and did it for a while.

It was at that point that I started drinking heavily. I was going through a fifth of Tanqueray a day.

Chapter 10

My first road trip was everything – I was making it to Miami and back in one day. I would get my best friend to ride with me most times, when I was only going for a day trip. At first, I let her think we were just riding down there to pick something up, but I ended up telling her what was up. And just like I thought, she was with it, especially since I was paying her for the ride. We tore the streets up – drop, shop, and back home. My son was always with my sister or my mom. I don't care what she did or what habit she possessed, she loved the hell out of her grandson. To this day, he has no clue who she really was; besides, what his dad would try to put in his head when he was mad at me…yeah, I know a peon move, all right. I was definitely guilty of messing with one. That's an L I'm accepting. He stayed mad that I wouldn't put him on. I would never – and I never did, but that's a whole other story.

Going back and forth, I met a lot of people, but nobody like Tommy. Every time he saw me, he would try and talk to me, but that wasn't what I was there for. I had a time frame and a schedule to keep, so I curved him every time.

Tommy would not give up. I finally gave him my phone number on a trip I made alone. It was his lucky night because I had taken a later ride than usual, and it was on a Monday, so I needed somebody to chop it up with on the way back home. I had about a six-hour ride, and I swear we talked during about four of those hours. We learned a lot about each other, including the fact that our stories were similar – I mean, almost identical. To be honest, I really enjoyed talking to him. Everything was about me and he never once asked about my business. That was different for me – usually guys were just trying to get in and get put on. I mean I wasn't big time like that, but I was doing better than a lot of people who claimed they were eating.

I found out that Tommy definitely wasn't hating – he was really The Man. He hated the fact that I was not going to school or working a nine to five. He hated it so much that he offered to buy me out. I laughed, but he was dead serious. "Why me?" I would always ask him. He didn't know it, but my self-esteem was shot to hell. It seemed to me that everything I really wanted never wanted me. What I didn't know was that what I wanted wasn't what I needed, and half the time, they were intimidated by me anyway. He would always have the perfect answers and they all made sense. He never tried to push up on me or treat me like anything less than a lady. We just mostly talked. We became long-distance best friends.

Chapter 11

"Get up!" was all I heard when I answered my phone at seven in the morning. I had a certain ringtone for him, so I knew exactly who it was when my phone rang. The only thing was, it couldn't have come at a more awkward time. I mean, we lived miles apart – I respected him and he respected me, so I knew there had to be something up for me to get a call at that time of morning without a heads-up the night before. I really hadn't talked to him at all over the past week, which wasn't out of the ordinary.

"What you mean 'get up'? Do you know what time it is? Why are you calling me this early? What's wrong? Oh, you must be in some-body bed or somebody in yours." I kind of laughed it off, although what he was saying couldn't have been more true. I had people that I talked to, but nothing was nothing was ever serious with me. I just didn't trust people, and I had been hurt, so I never wanted to experi-ence that again. To make sure it didn't happen, I built a wall so high only God could bring it down.

"I'm here and I want to see you."

"You here? What you doing here?"

"I wanted to see you, so I came down for the week."

I was smiling from ear to ear and by that time my company was looking like he was looking, and I was not even really concerned at that point. I was thinking of what I need to say to get him gone as soon as possible. Before I had the opportunity to exercise the lie, his phone rang and he had to leave.

An hour later, my doorbell rang. Let me tell, you I moved fast. I've always kept a nice, clean house, so there was nothing to get together but myself. He came in looking around, nodding his approval. I didn't have a TV in my living room. I was never in there, or even home, to be honest, so I didn't need one. He thought differently and put that as the first thing on his list to get me – cool, it was his money. We sat down, chopped it up for a little bit, made plans, and were out the door. It was nice having him down. We went out with my fam and his people, fam looking crazy because he was trying to figure out why this nigga was down here. He wasn't buying it that he came to see me and I wasn't either, but we would let it play out. There was no question about his loyalty – we had all been dealing for a long time. It was just quite odd because our home was somewhere he vowed to never be, but he had made good on his word for the last five years.

He said something else that night that was extremely odd: he started talking about relocation. The look on my face was priceless. As he talked, he was so tickled; I wasn't. I was really trying to figure out what the hell was going on. We got done eating and went to hang out on the beach for a while. Everybody made plans to link up, and we all went our separate ways. Tommy let me know that morning that any plans I had for the week needed to be canceled because he would be staying with me. I couldn't do that: I had a run I needed to a make and it couldn't be canceled or rerouted. But it was – what he said went, so I did it. That night, we went to bed just as soon as we shut the door. He was tired from driving and I was tired from sleeping. The next few days would be interesting.

It was different having a man in my bed, especially one I had grown to love in a way that I had loved no one else. It was like he just got me. It was night two when he finally made a move. I was nervous as hell, but ready. He was athletically built, standing at about 6'2", weighing 240 pounds, dark-brown skin, clean-cut, and smelled so damn good. Everything was going well until he told me to cut the lights on. "Cut the lights on? What you mean?" We went back and forth for about ten minutes. I guess you know, them lights came on, and when they did, my mood was killed, and I was under the covers. It was after that night that the wall came tumbling down. He made me get up and stand in the mirror. I wasn't naked, but I was barely clothed at that point. I was about 5'2" and about 210 pounds. Today I am fine as hell, but back then, I was the biggest one in my clique and I didn't like the way I looked at all. Although, you wouldn't know it just looking at me.

He stood behind me and pinched my stomach, which I thought was so big. He asked me, "Is this the part of you that's making you hide from me? "Is this what you don't like?" Before I could answer, he said, "I hope not, because this is the part that I love about you." he grabbed my breasts. "Is it these? Because I love these too. You never smile. Why?" he asked. "I rarely see it, but I love when you do it."

I couldn't even respond. Everything that I hated about myself, he pointed out and told me how much he loved that part of me. He made me feel okay about every insecurity I had. That night, all I could do was cry. That was the first time I had ever made love to a man. He loved every inch of me, especially the parts that I didn't like. After four days of this, I was in love, but just like all good things, it came to an end. During those four days, I made a promise to go back and school finish and never get on the road again. If I obliged, he would make sure that I would never want for anything, and he did just that.

Watching him leave was one of the hardest things I ever had to do. He promised he would be back, and he kept his promise as long as I kept mine. It was like we had become inseparable.

I met his family. His dad kept saying that there was something about me, and that time would reveal just what it was – he assured me that it wasn't a bad thing. He kept saying I was too good for his son, and to not get too wrapped up in him because he did not want to see me get hurt or waste any of my life. Tommy was ten years older than me, but I kept up with him as if I was just as mature as he was. He had one child – his daughter. She was mad cool. She liked me the first time we met. That was a relief.

His sister and her husband were mad cool, too. They would say the same thing as the dad. They assured me there was no other woman but warned me to be careful, out of fear that I could waste years of my life. I didn't get it, and every time I asked him about it, he said we would talk about what they meant. I had no idea when the talk would ever come.

Chapter 12

The day of the talk was the worst day of my life. Now, Tommy told me everything – we were best friends before we were anything. I mean, we talked about my niggas, his whores, and everything in between. There was nothing a man – not even him – could pull on me because he had given me the game. So when he tried to come at me with these around-the-world scenarios, I saw right through the BS.

"What's up, Tommy? What is it that you need to tell me? Just spit it out."

I had butterflies in my stomach and my anxiety was at an all-time high. I was thinking he was about to say he was married or had some secret life or something, until he said it. I just went blank.

"I'm facing twenty years. I've been going back and forth with this case for the last three years and the lowest offer they are giving me is twenty fed time."

I was relieved and devastated at the same time.

"What? How in the hell could you not tell me this? You made me fall in love with you, to do just what I asked you not to do." I was pissed. "So when do you go back to court?"

"In two weeks."

"Two weeks? So that's why you've been spending so much time with me, because it may be the last time we spend. Damn, Tommy, when were you planning on telling me this all this shit? When were you going to give me a chance to decide?"

"I was hoping that you didn't have to. That's why I didn't say anything at first. Man, who knew that I would fall for the Trap Queen?" He had a way of making me laugh, but there wasn't a damn thing funny right then.

I was really upset and I was also scared. Scared that I was going to lose again. I should have known that this thing was too good to be true. I heard him saying something, but I was so drowned in my own thoughts that I didn't even hear him calling my name, trying to get my attention. After about two more attempts, I finally heard him calling my name.

"Did you hear anything I just said to you?"

"Not really. I heard enough – you facing twenty years, you knew it and didn't tell me, that's the gist of it, right?"

"What you don't understand is, I thought that I could beat it and that they didn't have anything. Man, I don't know how to deal with this, either."

"You deal with it by being truthful with the ones who in your corner. But then again, you were straight up with everybody but me."

As bad as this shit stung, it was just the idea of losing this nigga that made me instantly forgive him. And just like that, I was in his corner, willing to ride it out and see what was going to be.

Chapter 13

Two weeks turned into a whole year that they were able to hold the thing off. In that year, I did some things I never imagined I'd do in a lifetime. It was Tommy who taught me that I could have anything I wanted, one way or another, but more so the right way. He hated that anybody had even shown me the game and allowed me to be a part of it. I couldn't understand why either. I just chalked it up to me doing what I had to do, but he showed me that I was simply lazy. It was of the biggest arguments we got into. One thing about him: whether it made sense or not, he was going to say it. His favorite line was, "The truth hurts, but it helps." I hated the fact that he was right most of the time. "Lazy? What do you mean lazy?" Why did I ask that question? I wasn't ready for the answer, but it didn't hurt as much as it helped! I had a story much like everybody else's. It was simply what I decided to do with it that made me different. I didn't understand it then, but I would.

The day came when he had to go. Twenty years was what they tried to give him, but ten was what he got. Still too many! It was me and his daughter that he wanted to see last. His father and sister had already gone back to the car on turn-in day. Nobody ever suspected that we would even get this far – I know I didn't. He talked to his daughter, made her promises that we were both sure he would keep. And then it was my turn. What he said to me was something I least expected and was not willing to accept.

"Move on!"

I knew it was what he would say. He spoke briefly about it before and I tried to dismiss it by assuring him that I would be there for him no matter what. I knew in my heart that there was no way I could wait for anybody for ten years, but the way I felt about him, I was damn sure going to try. He was always going to tell you why he felt the way he did or said what he said, and this time was no different. He would rather see me go and be happy with someone who could give me what I needed, than have me torment myself by telling him that I've found someone else. He would rather me leave him today knowing that I loved him the way I did at that moment. I just couldn't understand, and I was still unable to accept. He simply kissed me walked away, and told me to be good, to remember everything that he said I didn't like, because that would be what I needed. That it will hurt less when I stop answering the phone as quickly, or as often as I did before.

In my mind, I would show him I would write like crazy and answer every call. I never received a call, and every letter was returned.

Chapter 14

Not taking any of the advice I had received, I found myself in a low place. it was a place I had never been before. You see, I was one of those people who prided myself on making a way out of no way. I mean, I was able to come up with some kind of hustle no matter what it was, but this time it was different, and my pride didn't help. I would send my son to my mom's and sister's place, just so he didn't have to couch hop with me. I refused to ask my mom if I could live with her. My sister had a boyfriend, so I wasn't going there, and my grandfather – well, that was out of the question. After the way I left, I'd be damned if he had to see me come back. I thought about asking a friend, but I wasn't going to do that, either.

I had family that I could ask. I knew I would be the talk of the family, but it was the only option I thought I had at the time, so I put my pride aside and asked if I could stay for a while. A while didn't last long, but it was long enough. I was at the place where I had had enough. It was one thing to have a stranger kick you in your lowest place, but kin – that's a different kind of pain.

The crazy thing was that the leaking link was the people of my kin. I had started dating this guy and his people started talking to my people. As long as there was a common denominator, everything seemed to run smoother, so that was the approach I took…until it was brought to my attention that I needed to haul ass, and fast. There were some real ones left – few and far between, but they were out there. I often thought about Tommy and about what he said. He would have been so disappointed in me if he could see where I was and what I had done, which was nothing.

As smart and capable as I was, I just couldn't seem to get over the hump. I was prideful, sensitive, envious, and plain lazy! That was a hell of a combination, as well as a recipe for disaster. I was wearing the hell out of it, so get out fast was what he said. "Why?" was the first question I asked, although he didn't go into detail. I definitely read between the lines. All he said was, "I didn't know family operated like this." I took it for what it was and hauled ass fast!

Chapter 15

God has a way of doing things that I just can't understand.

I was always drawn to older people and them to me. All of my girlfriends were seven or years older than me or more. I had just met one when I went back to school to get my cosmetology license. She was living in a two-bedroom house – cute little place, just big enough for me and the kid. She just started telling me about it one day, and she was looking for someone to take over the rent, as she was getting married and moving in with her husband. I sat there without saying a word. I just listened to see if she would ask the million-dollar question.

And she did! "Do you know anybody looking for somewhere to stay?"

Before she could finish, I said, "I do."

"Really?"

"Yes, really. What do I need to do, move in, just like that?"

Now, I thought, something may not be right about this.

"Yes, my uncle owns the house, and he said if I find someone, he would let them move in. He just doesn't want the money to stop."

Now, one thing I didn't ask was how much the rent was going to be. I was so outdone when she told me the amount:

"$550.00."

"That's all? Oh, I can handle that!" I did enough hair to cover that and the bills, so I was straight. She said it was just that easy. I was gone in the next couple of days – didn't even leave a note. All I left was the key. It was said there was rejoice at my leaving, but I didn't witness it for myself, so I didn't feed too much into it. If memory serves me correctly, though, that was about right.

Things were going well. My boy was back home I was still in school. I wasn't working, but I was a hustler at heart, so I maintained above-average grades, but again I was living for the nightlife. I had joined a motorcycle club, and we were hitting it hard. Every weekend I was here then the next day I was over there, and drinking had become my new thing. I was still miserable as hell – something was missing. no matter how many people I surrounded myself with, I was still lonely. I drank as soon as I woke up and didn't stop until I was asleep, only to get up and do it again. I literally drank until I almost killed myself.

"I have to use the bathroom," I kept saying over and over again. I really did, and if anybody knows about drinking, piss comes whether you are ready or not. For some reason, I thought the car had slowed down, and I opened the door to get out. I was a pro at peeing outside – I was a drinker I always had to go!

All I remember is hearing my name being screamed out and cars coming to a screeching halt. I opened my eyes and realized I had been dragged under the car for almost half a mile. All I could see was dark as I felt the piss rolling down my leg. The same piss I, for some reason, just couldn't hold.

"Damn, I didn't make it," was what I thought to myself.

It's dark and hell is hot, as they say, and at that moment, that was exactly what I felt. I heard my name being called again. I open my eyes and saw the back tires of the car two inches away from my face…one second more and the car would have run over me.

But God is right, right? I don't think I ever said it that night. Being pulled from under the car, I refused help and just wanted to get home. I was so drunk that I didn't even see the blood dripping down my legs or feel the pain. I just wanted my cup and my bed. Everybody was frantic and I was thinking it wasn't that big of a deal.

God was with me two times that night. The second part was when the police came. He left as fast as he got there. To this day, I don't know what Jackie, said but whatever it was, they went for it. I arrived home feeling good that night, but when I woke up, that was a different story. My whole body was stuck to the bed. The blood had dried to the sheets. Every muscle in my body hurt. I couldn't walk – I mean not even move.

That wasn't the half of it, though: I was alone. How in the hell was I supposed to get up? "First of all, get these sheets from being stuck to me!" I had hardwood floors in my house. I heard a car door close and my door open. I didn't know who was coming, but I was grateful. I heard my name being called. It was Jackie. I looked at the clock and it was 7 AM. What in the hell was she doing up so early?

I didn't know why, but yet again, the Lord was looking out for me. It hurt like hell to peel the sheets off the dried-up wounds that were again fresh, and to again say that I couldn't walk or move was an understatement. She helped me out – another grown woman! I couldn't understand it, but what was crazier was that I didn't want the help, even though I knew I needed it. Even in my weakest state, I wanted to be the one to say I helped myself! P.R.I.D.E is a silent and deadly killer.

It was Jackie, though. She refused to leave me there, and every request to be left there fell on deaf ears. I remember her saying, "You tried to kill me last night – almost giving me a heart attack thinking, that I had killed you. There is no way in hell I'm leaving you here." She was right, so I obliged. That was one of my longest recoveries, and to this day, I still haven't recovered from it. But I later reinjured myself in another way.

Chapter 16

Three months passed. As well as I was doing something, it was as if something was always in the cut, just waiting on me. It was like I could not just get ahead. There I was maintaining, doing everything I could to stay afloat, but it still wasn't enough. All the hair I was doing came to just about a complete halt. Every resource I had dried up. It was either the light bill or the rent, which one would I pay? I figured I could buy time on the rent. I was never late, and for the first month, it worked. I paid all the bills, but damn, it wasn't as easy as I thought to come up with that rent. For the second month, I didn't have another good excuse. Uncle landlord was very flexible, but after two months, flexibility had worn out. I was literally sitting at the bottom of what I already thought was the bottom.

The notice I hated to see was staring straight at me – it was the red-lined light bill. How in the hell was I going to pay it? I had stopped answering the phone days before because everybody wanted what I owed them, and I didn't have the money or the ability to get it. A few days later came the sounds I didn't want to hear: my air stopped running, the ceiling fan stopped, and the tv just went off. It wasn't a power outage on the street, but in my house. And it was hot as hell outside. Luckily, it happened during school hours and my son wasn't home.

The first thing I did was call my mom. I wouldn't dare tell her what was going on, but what I did tell her was that I needed my boy to come over for a few days. She would never, ever know the real reason why.

My mom had a way of making me feel like shit. The thing was, she didn't even know she was doing it. She just knew that it was what she thought I needed to hear. What she didn't know was that most of the time, a messed-up person already knows they were messed up, and sometimes it's in their best interest to not broadcast that shit. I made the call, and she gave me the answer I knew she would. I didn't even want to face her, so I asked her if she could pick him up, and she did.

Two days was all I had to figure something out, not because I needed to figure something out, but because in my mind, all I could think about was what would they say if they found out.

Here came Jackie again. For some reason, it was easier for me to talk to some friends rather than others – especially rather than family. By the time I called her to tell her what was going on, she was there with bells on! I don't know what she did, but just like that, the fan came back on, the tv was blaring again, and my air was once again pumping. I didn't just hang with any old people. We all knew how to do something (some legal, some not), but whatever it was, we did it, and we let you know what you needed to do to not get caught! That lasted for every bit of three months. There was no way I was losing that house. I didn't have anywhere else to go, so I sold my car, paid my rent up for a few months, and there I was smooth sailing again…or so I thought

My aunt – I mean my favorite aunt – had called me about traveling with her for an event that she needed to cater. I took the gig. That was another couple of hundred dollars I could come back with and get me another little piece of car. It was spring break, so it was perfect timing: I could take my boy with me. That was perfect.

I was winning again. I went down south for two weeks, and as we all know, when there is an absence, there is trouble. It was just like school: you're gone for two days, come back, and all hell breaks loose.

Chapter 17

I pulled up to my house, and something was different. I knew I didn't leave my door open, and nobody but me had a key to my house, so why in the hell was my door open? I got out of the car and proceeded to the door very slowly. As I walked up to the door, I saw everything in disarray: my furniture moved all around, my refrigerator opened, I mean everything was just ransacked. I finally went all the way into the house and saw they had been through everything but took nothing. What the hell were they looking for?

We called the police. Who the hell showed up? The very officer I always had a run-in with. Before he got out, I saw him just shaking his head. We knew each other very well. The first thing he said was, "What the hell you up to now? I thought you were on the right track." It pissed me off, but how could I be mad? He knew me. Not saying anything besides are you here to do a job or…

He went in and came out with the same conclusion I had come to: somebody was looking for something. They had kicked my back door in and came out the front. Of course, nobody saw anything. That's the way I moved. I always stayed ducked off where I couldn't be easily seen, so I know nobody saw them and that they had apparently been watching me. Damn, back to square one. "I have to move again, but where am I going? Not this shit again!!!"

"You can always come to stay with me" was what I was heard on the other end of the line. Yeah, I could, but I really didn't want to, so I didn't. A week passed. That's how long it took me to get out of that house, find a place to store my stuff, and figure out a plan.

The last day I was at the house, something just came over me. I remember sitting on the floor and just talking to God. What started out as regular conversation ended in rage and tears and a lot of broken shit. I was angry, angry at God. I was like, man, I'm trying. I tried to fly right, but around every corner it was something. I was like, "What the hell do you want from me?" Thank God He is not like man, because I was talking real savagely. Unbeknownst to me, that was just what He wanted. I cried and screamed. I just couldn't understand how He was there for everybody else but kept forsaking me. I remember saying the words, "I'm tired, I want something new." I was tired of the same old things and getting the same old results. "If you are real like you say you are, and got all the power, then help me!"

Just like that, the rant was over. I was off the floor and out the door, face wet with tears. I just began walking, not sure where I was going. I just needed to get the hell out of there.

One month later, I got exactly what I asked for: everything new. That old saying "be careful what you ask for" was so true – my mother had agreed to pay my storage bill for me until I could get back on my feet.

I received a letter in the mail that said I had lost everything. There had not been a payment and the amount they needed, I didn't have. Honestly, I just didn't care. I was over it and I just didn't have a care to give. Of course, I brought it to my mom's attention, but she wasn't moved. It wasn't her stuff, and to hear her tell it, she just didn't have it. I didn't even have the energy to argue the fact that she didn't even tell me she didn't have it, so maybe I could have saved my stuff. But I also didn't have the energy to ask why the hell she agreed to pay it, and you know, she just really didn't give a damn. It was just evidence that God had to be mad at me and just wasn't fooling with me, period.

Chapter 18

Again, I was back at square one. I didn't have anything but the clothes I had not put in storage myself. My son and I ended up staying with my best friend for a while. I became depressed as hell. It wasn't for anything that she had deliberately done, but because I was in this situation. For the life of me, I just couldn't understand how the hell I went from way up top to rock bottom, just like that. Most of it was me and the way I thought, but my maturity level wouldn't let me see it at the time.

I always got mail at my mom's house. I used her address for everything and always, no matter where I lived or where I was. She had been calling me for weeks, telling me I had mail; but hell, I wasn't in a rush to get it…what the hell was it, besides bills? I finally caught up with her and got a bag full of mail. Just as I thought, it was all bills, except for one letter, addressed to me but with no return address – just a correctional department stamp. I knew exactly who it was from.

I was still confused, though, so it took me almost a week to open it. All kinds of emotions and questions ran through my mind. First, why the hell was this person writing me now, when my every attempt at reaching out to them had been rejected? Second – an even bigger question – what the hell did they want now, after two whole years of no contact??

"You have to be kidding me," I thought. Did this nigga have eyes on me? How the hell could a person so many miles away, who I no longer kept in contact with, know my every move and what was going on? Then the nigga had the audacity to say he was so disappointed in me but knew me well enough to know that I would bounce back. I had seen an unfamiliar number calling me, but I refused to answer it. That was just the way it was: I never answered unknown numbers, no matter how many times they call.

I came to find out it was his father calling me. After about a week or so, I finally reached back out through email. It was bittersweet. All the feelings I had came rushing back as if they never left, but I was a hardass and he knew it. Things could never be the same. A part of me felt betrayed, but then another part of me understood. I was more familiar with the feeling of betrayal, so that's the side I stayed on. Our communication to this day is still off-and-on, but it will never again be like it was. I called his dad, who was like a breath of fresh air. I wouldn't take anything that he offered – my pride wouldn't let me. He would always say, "You were and always will be one hell of a woman. You so damn bullheaded and strong. It's going to be your downfall one day." It took me almost forever to understand what he meant.

Searching for a job took me every bit of three years. I know that seems farfetched, but it's true. One thing about me: I was never going to be around a person getting a bag, and I wasn't going to get myself one, either. I had many hustles and I began to use each and every one of them. I always did hair, so I was doing hair all day, selling plates on the weekends, and talking good shit in between.

It was all streams of income, but I was tired of watching and listening to people talk about what they thought was the good life. I had lived far past what they were even just being introduced to, but what the hell could I say? Compared to before, what I was doing wasn't shit. I made up in my mind that not another day was going to go by where I was just mediocre. I applied and applied and applied. I couldn't find a Job ANYWHERE! I was so eager to get out of my situation that I swallowed my pride and went to McDonalds. I lived on the north side, but I applied to a location in Mandarin – a twenty- or thirty-mile difference. I'll be damned if they were going to see me flip any burger or drop any fry, but I was willing to do anything at that point.

I got a call-back and went to the interview – blew it out the water. I just knew I was going to get that manager position…NOT! I was informed that, after careful consideration, they thought I was a great fit, but with my experience, I was overly qualified. They were hiring for long-term, and they were sure that I would easily find something better and leave them as soon as another opportunity came along. Well I'll be damned, I just got curved by Mickey Ds!

I left there with tears in my eyes. I could not believe it. I actually set my pride aside, only to get a damn turndown. I was just outdone. And to think – I had no car and was talking to somebody that made my skin crawl just to get there. "I had to endure you talking to me a whole thirty minutes, then you had the nerve to want a hug? Nigga please, if you don't get yours." He didn't deserve that, and I would've been pissed to even think of the idea of someone doing it to me. At the time, though, it was what it was, and I wondered why I was going through all that. Looking back now, I can say that I deserved it.

Chapter 19

Back to the basics is what I called it. I was right where I started, but anxious to get farther. I couldn't get a job to save my life. I eventually decided, "Well, maybe I'll just return to school." I went and signed up, thinking I would just chill and get another degree. That worked for a while.

Getting back into school was a breeze, but that was to be expected. I went to a private school on purpose – you know, the kind that will admit you and get you financial aid, classes, and books in one sitting. Basically, all you had to do was sign your life away. What the hell, might as well. It didn't look like anything was coming of it anyway, but I was optimistic.

I started school that following week. Being who I was, it was no surprise that I could pass easily and get as many scholarships as they would allow me to get – that is exactly what I did.

The President's List was a standard for me, and I met it every semester. One semester, I only made the dean's list but that was cool; I was still in the top of my class. I always gave it my all.

Keeping up with the standard that I set for myself also ensured that I would receive my financial aid and additional scholarships, which was one of the reasons I even decided to go back. I'll be honest – I wasn't working, and I had a hell of a lot of pride. I was looking for a come-up anyway I could get it, so why not kill two birds with one stone?

I crushed for as long as they allowed me to. I was the one who would always stop the ball from rolling. I think I was afraid of success. I was so used to defeat, disappointment, and rejection, so that was all I knew how to work with. Anything else was new to me. Not knowing how to control it, I always resorted to what I could, which was the latter.

My living arrangements were very shaky, so it was time for me to get farther than where I was living, too. That place was the straw that broke the camel's back. I remember calling down to our local homeless shelter on many occasions, trying to get my name on the list. I was willing to go anywhere other than where I was. In my mind, I would go there I didn't know anybody, so what the hell? I found a program that would help you get on your feet. I called and called – no answer, I left message after message – all went unreturned.

Job hunting again. It was a devastating process. Around every corner, there was a rejection – one "no" after another. I was just about to say forget it and call my grandfather. Of course, I would have rather lived on the street than to have to go back and face him, just to hear him say "I told you so".

Just as I was about to throw in the towel, I saw an ad for Golden Corral. There WAS a God. In my mind, I knew that they had to be paying a decent amount. I did know that all of their food was made from scratch, so I applied. To my surprise, I received a callback the same day – actually, within a few hours! I was interviewed the following day and got the job.

This is where the BS comes in: the starting pay was only eight dollars. Eight freaking dollars! I was in no position to turn down anything. It was better than no dollars, so I took it. I decided that I would just work as many hours as I could. I let the manager know that I was available around the clock. That was all before I knew exactly what I would be required to do.

Now, that job and school wouldn't mix, and I knew that, but I still tried it anyway. I went on to psyche myself up, as if I would just take a break from school and then return. I knew that was a lie, but it was what I told myself anyway. I was ready to get out of the situation I was in.

I could always hear my favorite aunt's voice in my head: her answer to everything was "Just Pray." So I did. First, I needed to apologize, because the last time I had talked to God, I acted like a damn fool. He didn't even operate in the manner I thought He did, I would later learn. Eight dollars an hour and a prayer were all I had.

Later, I walked into the admissions office and talked to a counselor. I told her that I was going to be taking a leave of absence. Of course, she wanted to know why. I told her I needed to be working to get my son and me a place to stay. She listened to all I had to say. I have no idea why I was so compelled to tell her my story, but I did, and she acted as if I was such a strong person. I'm looked at her like, "Ma'am, all this on me is the reason I'm at this place." She kept saying, "You are so strong. So many people would have given up by now." In my mind, I was saying, "I've given up more than the people you are talking about I'm sure, but if you say so." That was my first lesson that not everybody sees you the way you see yourself.

The lady I had previously spoken to had sent word for me to come back to her office before I headed home that day. I was wondering what she could have wanted. When I heard what that was, I was surprised, but not shocked. She was so touched by my situation. She passed me a piece of paper and said to call one her friends. They had a property that was for rent, and she was sure they would let me get it. I was excited, but I didn't hold my breath – nothing this easy ever came to me or happened for me.

I called the number as soon as I got out of the building. I was anxious to see what it was about. The phone went straight to voicemail. I left a message, but I wasn't going to hold my breath over a callback. To my surprise, the call came almost an hour later, and it was a familiar voice on the other line: it was the same lady I had just spoken to about requesting the leave of absence!

"What the hell kind of game is she playing?" was what I thought. For one thing, I didn't mention was that my trust was all messed up, so I didn't trust anybody…or anything they had to say until I saw it. She went on to explain that she had to use "the friend verbiage" because she was the owner of the house and she didn't want anyone in the office to figure out what was going on. That made sense.

Chapter 20

The house looked like a sugar shack – and that was giving it too much credit. She said it needed a little bit of work…I don't know what she thought "a little bit" meant, but it definitely wasn't what I was looking at. It was evening in the dead of winter, so I gave it the benefit of the doubt and waited until early the next morning to come back. NOPE – same look, same thing. She met me there with the key.

Now, I won't lie, the house had potential. But who wanted to do all that? I had thought I was moving into a house that was ready. I mean, cleaning was inevitable, but this, looked more like reconstruction. It was three bedrooms, one bath – nice house, but DAMN!

We talked numbers. I just wasn't moved, especially with the deposit, so I made her a deal: I would clean the house and fix it up, paint and all. The only thing I needed her to do, I thought, was put in carpet and redo the kitchen floor. To my surprise, she agreed – too fast, it seemed, but it was an agreement. For the next couple of days, I cleaned and painted, and just as promised, she had brand new carpet installed and the kitchen floor redone. After about a week, the house looked brand new. A guy came to fix the garage and to paint the outside of the house. I was finally able to see some light at the end of the tunnel.

On moving, day I was so excited. It had been a long time coming. I and one of my friends moved everything I had into that house, which was NOTHING – I had a bed and a T.V. That was it. But so what? I was in my own shit and that was all that mattered. The first thing I wanted to do was fix my son's room up. I didn't care too much about myself, but he had all these ideas for his room, and all I wanted to do was make him happy.

The first night we stayed in the house was crazy. It was early spring in Florida, and that could feel like winter or spring – you never know. That particular spring was still cool, so I looked for the thermostat to cut the heat on and knock the chill off. There was no thermostat. Actually, I didn't even see any vents. What the hell??

She got me. That's why she was so quick to take me up on the offer of killing the deposit. There wasn't any heat and air in there, It was around 9 PM, but I didn't care – I called anyway. The first lie was her son was coming to put the thermostat in that weekend, but she would bring me a fireplace in the meantime. I obliged.

One weekend turned into fifty weekends. It was summer before I knew it, and she was bringing window units with an excuse. It didn't matter to me at this point. I had made it through winter, and the fireplace she brought actually worked. Little did she know, all this was working in my favor: I took one hundred dollars off the rent until she got it fixed. I was raised without central air and heat – I hated it, but I knew how to adjust. She finally got her son there a whole year later. He did a half-ass job, so my light bill kept being sky high. "Whelp, I still need the hundred off the rent until its fixed."

I was making it, and things were going pretty well, but I still didn't have a car. Income tax season was right around the corner. I had so much debt and owed so many people. That said, I didn't have to pay them back – I know that sound crazy. I needed the help I was getting, but there was no way I wasn't going to give it back. I couldn't take another "what I did for you". (Whether you were looking to get paid back or not, you were getting it.)

I should have gotten a car, but I couldn't. What I have yet to disclose was that during that whole process, I had been running from a warrant I had issued three years prior. I was on felony probation and was arrested again. That didn't violate me; what did was when I received misdemeanor probation and violated that one. That messed me all up. When I did that, my motto was "they would have to catch me" because I wasn't going back. I had managed to lay low for three years and counting. I was getting tired, but I couldn't be taken from my son again. This would be my third violation I knew I was going to be hid this time. I couldn't take that risk. I had only been out two years before I had violated again.

I needed another job. I was tired of only having enough to pay rent. I might as well have been a clown, I was juggling so much. It was Christmas Eve when I got the job at Applebee's. I was experienced, so this one paid a whole lot more. I was making twelve dollars starting out there, and a raise in ninety days. I was happy about the job, but I had no idea how I was going to get there. I worked from 9-5 at Golden Corral and six until closing time at the other. Closing time was 2 AM and we didn't leave until 3:30, if we were lucky.

Who came to get me at those hours? I had a few loyal friends that made the drive, and I was so appreciative. They were riders, though, so I expected nothing less. No matter how a person felt about me or what they thought, I was always considerate and respectable, so after a while I wouldn't let them come and get me. I just made a way. I either caught a cab or paid a co-worker going that way. There came a time when the rides just became too much. I was spending too much money, so I decided I would just catch the bus. I didn't realize that no bus ran that late.

Chapter 21

On my first night at the bus stop, security kept riding. I was working out of a huge mall, so I'm sure they were wondering what the hell I was doing out there. One night, somebody finally asked. He pulled up to me and asked me if I knew that the next bus wouldn't run until after the sun came up. I assured him that I knew. There was something about the way he said it that caused me to burst out in tears as soon as he left – like "What the hell has my life come to, that I'm sleeping outside at a bus stop for five hours a night until the next bus comes, only to have enough time to go home, shower, and catch the next bus to job number one?"

This went on for about three months. I still stayed at the bus stop overnight, but I had to let my first job go. I was going nonstop, and my body just couldn't take it. Besides that, I was forcing my son to have to grow up to fast. He was only eleven years old and he already knew how to catch public transportation home by himself, fix him something to eat, and go to bed without me being there. I would meet him in the morning, only for us to walk back to the bus stop together. I would put him on one bus and I would get on another, going in the opposite direction.

I had to quit. It was taking a toll on him more than it was on me. It was income tax season again. Damn that. I was still running, but I had to get myself a car. I don't know how I talked my mom into getting my car in her name, but I did. I think she felt sorry for me. I didn't give a damn – a yes was a yes.

I was a craigslist shorty for three days straight. I heard, "Look for a Lexus, look for a Lexus." Man, I had Buick money. I looked anyway, and I saw a 2011 GS300 for $1999.99 I thought, "This some BS," but I messaged the guy anyway. He said it wasn't a gimmick, and that the price was so low because he wanted $7,000.00 but it was broken in two and the window was broken, along with all the radio and speaker equipment gone. It was previously his son's car, and he had just graduated college, so he received a new Camaro as a gift. It needed a radio and a window, so he dropped the price. I ended up talking to this man for about two hours on the phone. By the time the conversation was over, he told me he would only sell the car to me and to bring him whatever I had.

I had what he was asking, but when I got there, he would only take half of it. He said that God told him to do it. I'm not sure what God told him, but I got the hell out of there before God told him to do something else. From the look of things, he was well off and didn't need any dime I had.

My Mom kept to her word and put the car in her name, so I was riding and had a decent piece of job and a place to stay. I was winning, but I wasn't. I was still ducking and dodging and hiding and running. I don't care what they tell you or how it looks, that's a miserable way to live. Now, I lived in the heart of the hood, so when I pulled up with a newer model Lexus, and these people knew they had just seen me on this corner the morning before, I got a lot of stares. The way I stared back, I think they knew to ask NO questions! I had twenty-two-inch rims, too, so I would always park my car in the garage behind the gate and lock it. I was taking NO chances.

Of course, things wouldn't stay good forever. Mom started tripping, and before I knew it, I chunked that tag at her ass. It wasn't right, but it was what it was. I was not one for anybody holding anything over my head. Hell, I knew what to do, and I did it. I was riding the next day.

It was around that time I had been encountered by so many people asking how I had gotten from where they met me to the place I was now. Of course, never giving myself any credit, I chalked it up to just knowing how to make it, and before I knew it, I was giving them just what they needed to get to the next step. I heard someone say you need to turn this into something – I heard it but dismissed it, until I was talking to a friend that introduced me to the nonprofit world. I thought, "Yeah, I might," and left it parked right there. All night, I thought, "Could I really? Nah nobody will support me." What people didn't know was that as much as I was on the bus or downtown, I spent most time talking to and helping people. so just maybe I could. I went for it, and I was still running.

Chapter 22

Things were going pretty well. The idea of having my own business rang in my ears, day in and day out. I was going to go for it! I planned my first event, just to introduce what I was doing to the masses. It was such a flop, nobody showed up. I was so hurt – devastated, really, especially by the fact that there were so many promises made. I didn't know that this came with the territory. I should be glad that I was experiencing my disappointment early; well at least part of it. It bruised me. I mean, it bruised me badly. I parked that car and wouldn't pick it back up for a while.

Work had become my top priority. I didn't do anything but that. I met a guy there. I never gave too many guys the time of day, but everything was going well, so what the hell, maybe I could entertain someone.

And so I did. He was such a kind soul. He was just what I thought I liked: he was dark, clean cut, had a foot ball player build, and he was a tad bit older than me. I said I wouldn't mess with anybody who was less than average. I didn't find any faults in him for the first couple of weeks. My son kept saying small things were missing, but we chalked it up to being lost and we just replaced it – until one day, when I couldn't find my keys.

Now, I sat my keys in the same place every day, and I knew where I had left them. How in the world could I suddenly not find them? He helped me look for them and assured me that he would stay at the house and find them. The next morning, I still couldn't find them. Before I went to work, I said to myself, "If this nigga all of a sudden just finds my keys, we have a problem." Just like that, he found my keys, so I told my manager I had an emergency and had to go home. He was gone by the time I got there, but so was my son's new PlayStation, his chain, and all his fitted caps. That nigga really had robbed me. What he didn't was that he had dropped his wallet What luck!

One thing I hated was a damn liar, but I despised a thief. I was on his ass and he didn't even know it.

I pulled up to the address, which was different than the one he had taken me to before. It was a very nice house: gate out front and all. I rang the bell to get in and a lady answered the bell. She asked for my name and I gave it to her. Sounding surprised, she asked who I was looking for and I told her. She then proceeded to tell me that was her husband and asked me what I wanted with him. She had more questions than I did. That gate came open so fast, and I went in just as fast. I really didn't give a damn about her questions. I had one thing in mind, and that was getting back what belonged to me. She was at the door even quicker and she had an attitude.

Before she could even get the attitude going, I asked, "Where is your husband?"

"He at work. Who are you, though?"

"Oh work, huh, that's what he told you. Nah, baby, he not at work. He out stealing people's shit."

In the background, I see a little boy around nine years old. I knew him to be his nephew, but I came to find out he was his son, and the lil nigga had on my son's necklace. Before I thought, I just reacted and snatched it from around his neck. She was slow before – she had time to react.

I was in the house looking for all my stuff. She was screaming at me to get out of her house and asking what was going on, all at the same time. I slowed down enough to tell her that I was messing with her husband and he had stolen all my son's things. Looking to the left, I saw a game plugged in. I grabbed it – it wasn't even the same kind of game, but I could only see red. What stopped me was the word, "Police!"

I froze and finally took a minute to hear what she was actually saying. "All I want to know is what's going on." I told her. She cried, but I was still scanning to see if I see my baby's shit. I didn't, so I left.

That's the short version. On my way out, I saw the police coming in. I was gone by that point. They lived off a dirt road, so when I got to the end of it, I hit it.

I was pissed. I couldn't believe that had just happened to me. That was some TV-type of stuff. I'm telling you, I couldn't pick them to save my life! That was a bullet I dodged. I never saw or heard from him again.

Chapter 23

Going on with life as usual, everything was going cool. Until I was riding down I-95 on my way to work and saw every bit of fifteen state troopers along the highway, pulling random cars. I slowed down, my heart practically in my feet. It was 2015 and that warrant had been signed since October of 2010. I was so tired of running, I was just like, "It is what it is."

As I reached the roadblock, I saw a lady officer standing out in the road. "SHIT," I said to myself. But to my surprise, she waved me on and stopped the car behind me. It was at that point that NOBODY could tell me that God was not real I cried all the way to work. That night, that I decided I could no longer live like that…and that I had to do what I had to do.

A family meeting was called between me, my sister, my mom, and my best friends. I told them what I planned on doing. I was going to call my lawyer the next morning and just go through with it.

The next morning came faster than any other morning had ever come. I was still firm on my decision. I called my lawyer – he was surprised to hear my voice. He didn't know what had happened to me. He knew I wasn't in jail, but he didn't know where I was. (The funny thing was, he didn't come looking, either, but that was neither here nor there. I was ready to get down to business.) Never in his twenty years of being a lawyer had he ever seen anybody fully functional while eluding the law for that long. I asked him if he believed in God. He said if he didn't, he darn sure did now.

He instructed me to wait on him, and that he was going to work on it right away. It was two days before I heard from him. Those were the longest two days I had endured in a while. He finally called, and what he said threw me – like, literally threw me. The judge who had signed my warrant five years prior had died, and they were having a hard time finding me. The warrant was still active, though. Of course it was.

After a few more days, he called with the news that he had found a judge to put me on the calendar. I was excited but scared as hell – the court date was a week out. I didn't know what to expect, and he was honest in saying he didn't, either, We discussed what he could propose, which was for me to pay all fines and him to argue the case that I had begun school, made attempts to start a nonprofit, and had not been in any more trouble in the past five years. Anything was worth a shot at that point.

The ball could also go the other way: I had been running for five years, and they could try to use me as an example. That was like a slap in the face. It also didn't help that the judge was one of the hardest on the bench. Even though he had no idea what the warrant was for, I was sure he would do his research. The charge held twenty-two years. I knew in my heart I wasn't doing that, but I wasn't sure if I would have to do the three years that I had on probation. Only time would tell, but either way, I was ready.

The week leading up to my court date, I prayed more than I had ever prayed before. I remember hearing a voice say, "You not going back to jail again." Now, I'll be honest, I heard it but dismissed it at the same time. I was actually looking forward to doing some kind of time – not a lot, but something. It was unheard of to elude for five years and then walk away scot-free, and I was a black woman. I was a prime example of the best example.

Preparing my job was also a tough thing to do as well "Will finding out my truth lead them to fire me?" Not! My manager was the coolest, and she loved me. I don't know how I had that effect on all people except the ones I wanted.

The day finally came. It felt like I was walking the green mile. I didn't want anybody to go with me, but my mom wasn't having that. She was going, come hell or high water. I remember counting each step on my way up to the courtroom that would hold my fate. My heart was pounding so fast. I was reciting the 23rd Psalm over and over again, followed by the 91st. I sat on the cherrywood bench just outside the courtroom. The bailiff came over and asked me my name. Now, I knew this man had no idea what I was there for, but to me, it looked as if he was already feeling sorry for me – like he knew what was going to happen. I was tripping, but hell, you would too, being in my position.

Chapter 24

I was checked in and lead into the waiting area of the courtroom. That judge was not playing. My mom was like, "Baby the cracker" – yeah, that's what she called him – "not playing. But I'm not either, and you not going back to jail."

I wanted to believe with her, but I was so conflicted. He wasn't giving anyone a chance to speak, and he was throwing time left and right. He was definitely on a roll. I was next. My knees felt like jelly as I approached the bench. I was walking slowly. My mouth felt like cotton and I had to use the bathroom. Looking at me, though, you wouldn't be able to tell any of that. I held my composure pretty well until it was time to speak. It was if my voice had left.

The judge asked me my name and I could barely get it out. He read my docket, and then he read it some more. He put it down. He said, "You know, I have been waiting to meet you all week, and I must say, you are nothing like what expected."

I was dressed to kill. If I was going in, I wanted to look good coming out. I don't know why I thought like that. I guess I just wanted to be prepared for anything.

"So let me get this straight. It has been five years since we have seen you. This place wasn't even here yet."

"Yes, sir," was all I could say, as if I was programmed.

He asked me, "So why are you even here?"

My lawyer proceeded to speak up, but the judge quickly told him he thought I was more than capable of speaking for myself. He said if

I had run for this long, he knew I had a high level of intelligence. He hadn't seen anything like this that often, either.

I can't recall everything that was said, but whatever it was, he was buying it. He asked me if I knew how serious of trouble I was in. I explained to him that I did. We talked for what seemed like thirty minutes before he even picked up my docket again.

"It says here that you have restitution for almost $7,000.00, but you only have a balance left of $113.00."

Now, I already knew that I hadn't paid one dime of anything, but if that's what his paper said, who the hell was I to correct him? Again, "Yes, sir" was all that I could mutter. In his eyes, it looked as if I had been paying somebody somewhere while I was running. I wasn't, but hey, I was going with it.

"So where were you going to pay without being seized?"

Thank God my lawyer was on point because I already didn't know what the hell he was talking about. I couldn't answer that question if I tried. As if he read my thoughts, my lawyer jumped in.

"I was making them for her, Your Honor."

The judge looked as if he knew it was a lie, but he went with it. He was quiet for about one minute, but it seemed like ten. He then asked me what I wanted to do, citing that I looked like a pretty decent young lady who had made some past mistakes and had already learned from them. He asked me again what I wanted to do. I shouted quickly and strongly. "I want to go home!"

"Now you can talk, huh?" he laughed. He said, "I don't know why I'm saying this, but if you can bring this balance to zero by tomorrow, I'll just see about that."

I ran out of that courtroom so fast. $113.00 – I had that in my pocket! I went to the first floor and paid the clerk. I asked her for not one, but two copies. I left one in the car and put one in my purse. I cried all the way home. I couldn't believe this man had just said he would let me go. Surely this was a joke and he would change his mind tomorrow.

There was only one way to find out.

9 AM court came quickly. I didn't even sleep. Sure enough, as soon as I walked in the courtroom, he called me up first. Again, I had jelly knees and a weak voice. This time, he didn't talk as much. He looked in his computer at what I assumed was the balance to see if it was paid. I was out quicker than I was in, just like he said. He let me go home, but not before telling me that there was something about me that told him he knew I wouldn't be back, and that he always trusted what he knew.

I was so grateful. I could not believe this was happening to me. I was FREE!

Coming from where I had just been, I knew the thought process and the reasoning of re-offenders. I was one, and I would do whatever I could to make sure that those serious about rehabilitation were looked out for. It was at that point that something beautiful came from something so ugly!

The Pivot started at the point I decided to get myself free at any and every cost. It was the very thing that pushed me to my next level!

The Next Level!!

I wanted to change everything about me. I said it again for the second time. You would think that I would learn about saying the wrong things, but wait – were they really the wrong things? I walked into the salon where my cousin worked and say the four magic words she loves to hear:

"Cut it all off."

"Are you sure? You know I never have a problem with cutting, but I want to make sure you are totally sure. Once I cut it, I can't put it back on."

Instead of saying anything, I took her shears and cut a huge chunk out of my hair.

"Oh yes, I guess you are sure!"

After about an hour of cutting and then coloring, I looked in the mirror and hated what I saw, but what the hell, I asked for it. Like everything else in my life that I hated, it seemed that everyone else loved it. I never said that I didn't like it or showed any emotion, either.

The next thing I said was, "Let's color it again."

"What?"

"Color it again. Yes, let's color it RED." It was a very bold move, but that was the exact way I was feeling, so I went for it.

The Lady with the Red Hair – what could she change next?

To order additional titles from Quiana:

ORDER FORM

Email form to: sisterandsampsonpublishing@gmail.com

(Please print clearly to ensure prompt delivery)

Ship to:
Mr./Ms./Mrs. _____
Street Address _____
Apartment Number/Suite _____
City _____ State _____ Zip_____
Telephone (_____) _____ - _____

PAYMENT METHOD

I've enclosed a Check/Money Order _____

WE PROUDLY ACCEPT
Credit Card: VISA ... DISCOVER PayPal

**Quantity and Book Title: Cost:
_____   PIVOT $20.00

*Taxes-add 7% tax to all orders   *add 4.95/book for shipping

Total Cost: _____

**Special discounts are available on quantity purchases by corporations, associations, educators, and others. For details, contact the publisher at the above listed address.

U.S. trade bookstores and wholesalers: Please contact Sister and Sampson Publishing

Email sisterandsampsonpublishing@gmail.com

About the Author

Ms. Quiana Malone holds many titles of responsibility, from founder/CEO to philanthropist – however, she feels her most important title is Community Servant. Ms. Malone is committed to serving the underprivileged and disenfranchised people throughout the United States by way of Grassroots Foundation and Process Implementation. Both organizations require involving the communities in which these individuals work, reside, and raise families.

Ms. Malone has a strong presence with a population of people who have not yet received their second chances. Her theory is, "Nothing about me without me." This short mantra shows that client buy-in essential, and so is the society in which we all coexist. Believing in transparency and accountability, she has adopted the technique of the Sunshine Law in her organization to ensure that legal, moral, and ethical standards are met.

Ms. Malone has been featured on many news outlets, speaking out against injustice all over the world, as well as voicing her support of rehabilitation support services to those who have sanctions against their records. She was a key feature in Essence Magazine's November 2018 edition.

Ms. Malone is currently working with other groundbreaking leaders throughout the United States to replicate the success of her first organization, **1 Step Up Jax**. She is also working to tackle issues that are systemically set up to create barriers based on socioeconomic class and status, education, poverty, and scarce resources.

To book Quiana for your next event:

sisterandsampsonpublishing@gmail.com

www.ingramcontent.com/pod-product-compliance
Lightning Source LLC
Chambersburg PA
CBHW060346050426
42336CB00050B/2146